I0531142

DELAYS, DETOURS, AND "I DO"

TRAVEL MISADVENTURES AND A PANDEMIC DESTINATION WEDDING (A SHORT MEMOIR OF RESILIENCE, DETERMINATION, TRUST AND LOVE)

ANNA SALDIVAR TURPIN

THE LUXE NORTH
—PUBLISHING—

Copyright © 2023 Anna Saldivar Turpin

All rights reserved.

The content contained within this book may not be reproduced, duplicated or transmitted without direct written permission from the author or the publisher.

By reading this document, the reader agrees that under no circumstances is the author responsible for any losses, direct or indirect, which are incurred as a result of the use of the information contained within this document, including, but not limited to, — errors, omissions, or inaccuracies.

ISBN: 978-1-998099-08-5 (Hardcover)

ISBN: 978-1-998099-06-1 (Paperback)

ISBN: 978-1-998099-07-8 (Ebook)

Legal Notice:

This book is copyright protected. This book is only for personal use. You cannot amend, distribute, sell, use, quote or paraphrase any part, or the content within this book, without the consent of the author or publisher.

Disclaimer Notice:

This work depicts actual events in the life of the author as truthfully as recollection permits. While all persons within are actual individuals, some names and identifying characteristics have been changed, some events have been compressed, and some dialogues have been recreated.

Published by The Luxe North Publishing

Montreal, QC, Canada

Enthusiasm is common. Endurance is rare.

— ANGELA DUCKWORTH

CONTENTS

INTRODUCTION

As I sit down to recount the extraordinary journey that led me to say "I Do," memories flood my mind like waves crashing on a shore. This memoir, *Delays, Detours, and I Do,* is a testament to the unpredictable path my husband and I took on our way to our marriage—a journey filled with unexpected twists, airport misadventures, and, most importantly, an unwavering love that defied all odds.

From the moment Keith and I met and got to know each other, there was an undeniable spark that ignited a love that would take us on a whirlwind adventure like no other. As we found ourselves deeply entwined in each other's lives, we knew that we were destined to share our future together. When the time came to plan our dream wedding, we decided to embrace our wanderlust and celebrate our love in a far-off destination, where the turquoise waters and golden sands would witness our sacred vows.

However, little did we know that our quest for a destination wedding would be far from smooth sailing. The universe seemed to have other plans for us, testing our resolve at every turn. Our journey began with flight delays that became a recurrent theme, much like the rhythm of a familiar song that refuses to leave your mind. Yet, as we stood in those bustling airport terminals, our hearts remained steadfast, grounded in the belief that love conquers all.

As we embarked on our first flight, excitement coursed through our veins, but fate had a different itinerary for us. The flight that was meant to take us to our connecting destination encountered mechanical issues, grounding us for what seemed like an eternity. Our patience was tested as we watched the minutes tick by, but we refused to let these challenges deter us. Instead, we held each other close, finding solace in knowing we have each other amidst the airport chaos.

From one airport to the next, we encountered a series of misadventures that could have derailed our dream wedding. Yet, like two intrepid explorers, we navigated through all the barriers with determination, unwilling to let these setbacks dampen our spirits, but instead finding humour in our journey. From lost luggage to airline mishaps to every detour, every hurdle brought us closer together, and our resilience deepened.

While recounting the events of this trip, I recall similar mind-boggling circumstances in the past. And so, I wanted to share those stories here as well.

We learned that the essence of true love lies not in a flawless journey, but in the way we faced the challenges together, hand in hand—a tapestry woven with threads of determination, trust, and unwavering commitment.

Delays, Detours, and I Do is not just a memoir; it is a tale of love's triumph over adversity, a testament to the power of two hearts beating as one. It is a reminder that love is not confined to the moments of perfection, but rather, it thrives in the face of imperfections and the unpredictability of life.

Join me as I take you on this incredible journey of love, laughter, and resilience—a journey that defied all odds and led us to say those two precious words: "I Do." This memoir is a celebration of love's unwavering spirit, and I hope that through our story, you find inspiration in embracing life's uncertainties with courage and an unwavering belief in the power of true love.

PART I

CHAPTER 1: TORONTO TO DENVER

F riday, August 6, 2021, marked a day of excitement and anticipation for me and my fiancé Keith. Our journey to the alluring islands of Hawaii from the usually bustling city of Toronto was about to commence. Toronto, along with the rest of Canada and the world, had only recently started to reopen and come back to life from the COVID-19 pandemic within the last few months, and we couldn't wait to travel again.

This wasn't going to be just an ordinary trip. My name is Anna and allow me to take you back to the previous year and tell you a bit first about how our incredible travel adventure came to be.

Over a year ago on July 25, 2020, a few months into the pandemic, Keith and I were at the cottage in Havilland Bay, a 30-minute drive north of Sault Ste. Marie, Ontario, where we spent our isolation days since April. It was a beautiful sunny day and we decided to get on our Sea-Doo personal watercrafts and enjoy a fun day out on Lake Superior. We rode off to a sandy beach on Batchawana Island, one of the few little islands nestled in the majestic lake just off the mainland.

Batchawana Island

The next thing I know, Keith proposes; I said yes, and we became happily engaged. If you're curious about how the proposal transpired, you can check out the video evidence online at bit.ly/annagotkeithed. Keith so cleverly planned out the whole thing without me suspecting a thing!

In the midst of uncertainty, we made a daring decision that would forever change our lives: we were going to get married in Hawaii! The world was in a state of flux, and no one could predict what the following year would bring with all the imposed limitations on social gatherings.

As we delved into the logistics of planning a wedding during a pandemic, we recognized that the rules and restrictions on gatherings varied from city to city. However, the silver lining was that these limitations seemed to align perfectly with what we wanted. You see, an overly large wedding with hundreds of guests was never really something we wanted to begin with. Something smaller, more intimate would be perfectly fine for us.

Now, I, coming from a mostly typical Filipino family, weddings tend to be celebrated with lavish festivities, and it is almost customary, or rather expected, to invite extended family members to join in the joyous occasion. That means it could easily tally up to *at least* 100 extended family members just from my side alone plus friends. Not to mention, Keith's family, originally from northern Ontario, isn't small either. Siblings, cousins, second cousins, plus their (mostly adult) kids would also be about 100 people from his side plus friends.

Hey, it's not that we don't love nor want our extended families to be there with us on our special day —the financial cost is an important factor to consider as we're the ones paying for our wedding ourselves after all. With no extravagant amount of money to spend and not wanting to drown in debt for the sake of fulfilling societal expectations, ultimately, the allure of a destination wedding beckoned us. It was the perfect solution—a serene escape from the norm, an intimate gathering of those closest to our hearts, and an opportunity to create amazing memories.

And truth be told, my introverted nature was another reason for wanting it to be non-local, too, as it's a setting where more comfortable connections could better flourish without me being overwhelmed by the multitude of faces around me.

Planning a destination wedding was like embarking on an exhilarating adventure, filled with dreams and uncertainties. I must admit that Hawaii isn't exactly an inexpensive place to have one. Our hearts (and pockets) were torn between the stunning landscapes of Lake Louise in Alberta, the enchanting allure of Whistler in British Columbia, the tropical paradise of Boracay in the Philippines, the idyllic shores of the Bahamas, and other captivating locations. Each place had its unique charm, and I meticulously kept track of every price quote on a spreadsheet, trying to find the perfect match for our once-in-a-lifetime celebration.

As the clock ticked, we had a little bit over 12 months to turn our vision into reality. Amidst the excitement, we faced the challenge of figuring out how many guests to invite. The pandemic cast a looming shadow of uncertainty, making us question every decision. But we embraced the journey with determination, finally settling on inviting 60-80 people, all the while holding onto hope that all those family and friends would join us on our special day.

Every step of the way, we had to adapt and adjust, making room for the unexpected. We accounted for more than we anticipated, just in case all the people we reached out to *did* decide to share in our joy. With each twist and turn, our hearts beat with anticipation, wondering how our wedding plans would unfold amidst the scenic wonders of our chosen destination.

Now, fast forward to that August day. As the early morning sun began to rise, Keith, eagerly awaiting the adventure ahead, was picked up by his Uber at 5:04 a.m. from his tranquil Humber Bay Shores condo in South Etobicoke, a suburb of Toronto.

Meanwhile, in the Alderwood neighbourhood where I lived at that time, I and everyone in my family —my parents, sister, and two brothers—were also getting ready that morning to soon leave for the airport.

Since it was only about a 10-minute drive from where Keith lived, we'd already planned ahead that Keith, with his Uber, was going to pick me and my sister up on the way to the airport, while my parents and two brothers were going to take a separate Uber.

And so, at 5:15 a.m., Keith and his Uber made a stop to collect me and my sister, from our apartment. It was a quick ride from there to the airport, especially as it was still early in the morning. Together, the three of us promptly arrived at Terminal 1 in Toronto Pearson International Airport (YYZ) at 5:25 a.m.

My heart leaped with anticipation as I looked around the airport to see where the line was to drop off our luggage for our 9:10 a.m. Air Canada flight AC1037/UA8639, a codeshare with United Airlines. This first flight leg was destined for Denver International Airport, Colorado (DEN) where we would have a short layover before getting on to the next flight leg to Hawaii. We got to the airport more than three hours before flight departure, so we'd have lots of time and should have no problem getting to our next destination on time... or so we thought.

Shortly after our arrival, my immediate family joined us at the busy airport and prepared to drop off their bags for their 8:00 a.m. flight to Los Angeles International Airport, California (LAX) where their layover was. Yes, arriving at the airport several hours before departure had become the new norm, an essential precaution during these uncertain pandemic times.

Upon reaching the check-in counter, we found

ourselves in a single line, regardless of our final destination. After securely checking in our luggage, we proceeded to the next line for the rigorous security check, which, much to our dismay, would not commence until 6:00 a.m. The airport staff swiftly redirected passengers based on the urgency of their flights, ensuring those with earlier departures were prioritized. It was at this point that Keith and I bid farewell to my family, knowing that the next time we'd see them was going to be in Hawaii.

Finally, after enduring the meticulous security and customs procedures, we reached our designated gate at approximately 8:15 a.m., with a mere 10-15 minutes remaining before the announcement of boarding. A glimmer of relief flickered within me as it seemed our flight was adhering to the schedule. Little did we know, this was merely the beginning of a day filled with unexpected twists and turns.

Shortly after all passengers were settled and secured in their seats on the plane, the pilot's voice resonated throughout the cabin, delivering news that dampened our spirits. The plane, it appeared, needed to await the arrival of passengers who were still in line at customs. Minutes turned into half an hour, and half an hour morphed into a frustratingly prolonged 45 minutes, marking the first in a series of disappointments that lay in wait. **Fail #1.**

Aware of the imminent impact on our connecting flights, the empathetic flight staff realized the urgency of the situation. With a heavy heart, the pilot finally conceded that further delays were no longer tenable. It was time to make a tough decision. Regrettably, the remaining passengers would not be able to join this flight. Their luggage, already loaded onto the aircraft, would soon be offloaded.

As the gate finally closed and the plane began its departure preparations, a collective sigh of relief echoed through the cabin. Keith and I, and the other passengers, found solace in the notion that our aerial journey was finally about to commence. However, our momentary respite was abruptly shattered when, a mere five minutes later, the pilot's voice reverberated through the intercom once again. The weight of his words hung in the air like an unwelcome mist.

"Apologies for the inconvenience, ladies and gentlemen," the pilot's voice crackled with a mix of frustration and concern. "We have encountered a mechanical issue that requires immediate attention." **Fail #2.**

Dismay washed over us, our minds filled with a tidal wave of disbelief. How could fate be so merciless? The plane had languished at the gate for an extended duration, seemingly ready to embark on its voyage, only for this unforeseen obstacle to emerge at the eleventh hour.

It was as if misfortune had intentionally conspired to test our resolve.

Engulfed in a sea of uncertainty, we glanced at our fellow passengers, each face etched with an amalgamation of disappointment and resignation. Conversations swirled with trepidation, whispers of missed connections and dashed expectations intermingling within the confined space. The palpable anxiety was a stark reminder of the intricate web of travel plans that had now unravelled before us.

"We're never going to make our connecting flights," a despairing voice murmured, punctuating the collective sentiment that hung heavy in the air. We nodded in sombre agreement, our hearts sinking at the realization that the meticulously orchestrated timing of our journey had been tossed asunder.

Yet, amid the gloom, a glimmer of hope materialized. The pilot's subsequent announcement, tinged with a sliver of relief, revealed that the diligent maintenance crew had swiftly addressed the mechanical issue. A mere ten minutes were all it took to rectify the hindrance that threatened to keep our plane grounded. While this small victory provided a momentary reprieve, it couldn't overshadow the fact that our carefully crafted travel plans had been dealt a severe blow. The shadows of failure cast a long, haunting spectre over our anticipated adventure.

As our plane embarked on its journey, we found ourselves faced with a daunting challenge. The lengthy three-hour and thirty-five-minute flight allowed us a mere five minutes upon landing to catch our connecting flight from Denver to Kona International Airport (KOA) in the sun-kissed paradise of Kona, Hawaii. I made sure I had my times right, keeping in mind that Denver is on Mountain time, two hours behind Toronto's Eastern time.

CHAPTER 2: DENVER TO HAWAII

Upon touchdown in Denver, the flight staff kindly requested passengers without connecting flights to allow those with pressing time constraints to disembark first. Eager to make the most of our limited window, Keith and I were among the first to rush off the plane, propelled by a mix of adrenaline and determination. The thought of boarding our connecting flight, even without our checked luggage, held a glimmer of hope.

Undeterred by the meager five minutes, we sprinted through the bustling terminal, making use of the tram to bring us to another terminal to get to our gate. My heart pounded in rhythm with our hurried steps, our breaths quickening with the realization that time was slipping through our fingers. Each passing second became a precious commodity, fueling our determination to catch the elusive flight.

However, as we arrived at the gate designated for United Airlines flight UA1758, our hopes were swiftly extinguished. The aircraft we had desperately hoped to board had departed earlier than scheduled, leaving us stranded in a blanket of frustration. United Airlines, unlike our previous flight, had not shown the same patience and consideration. The sight of the vacant gate cast a shadow of disappointment over our weary hearts.

To compound our exasperation, we soon discovered that there was only one flight from Denver to Kona that day. With no alternatives available, our plans to get to the island that day were deferred by an agonizing twenty-four hours. It was a disheartening turn of events, marking yet another failure in our tumultuous travel chronicles.

An air of urgency enveloped us as we rushed to the customer service counter, our hopes hinged on finding a solution to our disrupted travel plans. Rather than settling for a rebooking on the next available direct flight, which entailed an agonizing twenty-four-hour wait, we implored the customer service agent to consider alternative options within the Hawaiian archipelago. Our primary goal was to avoid the need for another COVID-19 test.

Our persistence paid off as we secured seats on the

1:55 p.m. flight from Denver to Honolulu (HNL), which, although was on a different island, will get us to Hawaii in time before our current COVID-19 test results expire. Eager to alleviate the discomfort of our prolonged journey, Keith graciously paid for business class upgrades, ensuring a more comfortable experience for me and him during the arduous seven-hour flight. With the details settled, we made our way through the Hawaii pre-clearance desk, obtaining the necessary clearance before making our way to the designated gate, where anticipation and relief came upon us.

During this period of waiting, remembering that United Airlines didn't have inter-island connections, Keith took the opportunity to book a new HNL to KOA flight with Hawaiian Airlines. This additional arrangement, while coming at an out-of-pocket expense of $177.80 USD, provided us with a glimmer of reassurance amidst the chaos of our travel tribulations. In the current overall view of things, this was just a minor inconvenience, and we were intent to get reimbursement from United Airlines/Air Canada for this at a later time, one way or another.

The in-plane selfie

As we finally boarded the plane, a sense of relief washed over us. I was brimming with excitement and I savoured the prospect of my first-ever experience in business class. The significance of the moment for me prompted me to, of course, capture it with selfies and a video, etching this milestone into our collective memory.

Alas, our hopes were quickly deflated as the flight staff relayed an announcement through the plane's intercom system. A hydraulic issue had been discovered, necessitating the prompt disembarkation of all passengers. The subsequent restart of systems meant the absence of air-conditioning, resulting in uncomfortably high temperatures within the cabin. Failure once again cast its shadow, marking another setback in our travel chronicles—**Fail #4.**

Returning to the gate, we patiently waited for updates, each one further prolonging our journey. At around 3:20 p.m., the disheartening news arrived: the maintenance crew had been unable to rectify the issue, prompting the dispatch of a replacement aircraft —**Fail #5**.

As a result, all passengers were redirected to a new gate, where we would board a new plane that will save us finally from all the waiting. The mounting failures tested our resilience, casting bumps in our no-longer-smooth voyage.

At the new gate, Keith and I found ourselves with disappointment once again—the absence of a plane. Our patience was tested once again as we waited. We had our hopes pinned on the elusive arrival of the eagerly anticipated plane. As the minutes ticked by, the gate staff delivered a disheartening update: the second plane, meant to alleviate our woes, had succumbed to its own mechanical breakdown while on its way to the gate. However, the gate staff assured us that a third aircraft was emerging from the maintenance hangar, promising respite from our prolonged ordeal. Yet, the recurring theme of failure continued to haunt our journey—**Fail #6**.

Enduring another agonizing wait of 15 to 20 minutes, Keith and I received the much-needed confirmation that a functional plane awaited us. A glimmer of hope was rekindled. However, this sliver of optimism was short-lived. Mere minutes later, the pilot's conversation with the gate staff resulted in a disheartening announcement: the plane no longer had a pilot available, having reached their designated hours for the day. After enduring countless delays, our spirits were deflated once again—the waiting had amounted to nothing. We were left with no choice but to be rebooked on a flight scheduled for the following day —**Fail #7.**

The toll of time weighed heavily upon us, as every passing hour brought us further from our thoughtfully planned trip. Our impending wedding, the raison d'être of our journey, loomed over our minds, magnifying the stress that had accumulated. Adding to our burdens was the stringent requirement imposed by Hawaii—the necessity of COVID-19 tests within a 72-hour window of the final flight leg. With the 24-hour delay, the precisely timed tests we took on Tuesday, August 3rd at 5:00 p.m. Eastern Time, would expire. Thus, we were compelled to shell out an additional $400 USD for new PCR tests, another unforeseen expense that further burdened our budget.

Relegated to the August 7th DEN to KOA flight, I briefly lamented the missed opportunity to utilize our time beyond the confines of the airport. However, the customer service agent, recognizing our predicament, sought to provide some solace. A hotel voucher, $80 worth of food and beverage vouchers, and two Lyft credits were offered as compensation. Furthermore, the agent graciously gifted us two United Airlines freshen-up kits, each containing a water bottle, towelette, mints, deodorant, hand cleanser, resealable bag, toothbrush, and toothpaste. Despite these small gestures, the bitter taste of disappointment lingered in the air, tainting our journey with an undeniable sense of frustration.

Fortunate enough to beat the closing time, Keith and I made our way to the COVID-19 test center nestled within the airport. With a mere 15 minutes remaining before they closed off at 6:00 p.m., we swiftly registered and underwent the nasal swab test. Miraculously, the results materialized within a mere 10 minutes, a stark contrast to the prolonged 24 to 48-hour processing times of the Hawaii-approved testing center in Canada.

Armed with $80 in food and beverage vouchers, we opted to indulge in a delectable dinner at Elway's, a renowned steakhouse nestled within the airport. As fate would have it, our server/bartender hailed from The Beaches area in Toronto, sparking a pleasant conversation. We shared our tale of unexpected airport misadventures, seeking insights on the optimal time to arrive the next day to avoid lengthy queues. Our newfound acquaintance suggested a buffer of 1 1/2 hours prior to departure, a helpful tip we were grateful for. The food experience surpassed our expectations, so, for future travellers and layover transit passengers, I recommend that you savour the mouthwatering steaks on Elway's menu.

Post-dinner, Keith and I ventured to the airport's designated rideshare area, determined to redeem our Lyft credits. However, a disheartening pattern emerged as time passed, as five minutes turned into twenty minutes. Despite the presence of several Lyft vehicles and a gathering of approximately 20 hopeful passengers, our ride requests on the Lyft app remained unaccepted. Perplexed, we pondered the unexpected turn of events, surmising that the drivers perhaps deemed their destination too close for convenience. As we engaged in conversation with fellow stranded travellers, we discovered that we had the same destination—none other than the hotel designated by the airline for overnight accommodations. It seemed others had been waiting for over 30 minutes, plagued by the same issue.

the fourth level of the sprawling hotel, its corridors seemingly stretching into infinity.

Upon arriving at our room, I confidently tapped the key card against the door, only to be met with an unresponsive lock. Undeterred, I tried the other key card, yet it yielded the same result. In a moment of sheer frustration, I made one final attempt, reversing the key card and pressing it against the door, but to no avail. All seemed lost until in a bewildering moment, the door handle began to turn on its own, and the door slowly swung open.

Wait, what?! Is this some mischievous supernatural being playing tricks on us?

Relief washed over us as we quickly realized it was not the work of a ghost or whatnot, but rather the same couple we met earlier at the airport emerging from the room. The reality set in—an unfortunate mix-up had occurred, with both parties being assigned the same room number. A shared sense of confusion permeated the air, signalling our impending walk back to the reception desk to rectify the situation.

Before heading back, I tried tapping the key card against the adjacent room doors in the hope or rather a desperate attempt that one of them unlocks, but alas, none of them worked so it wasn't simply a matter of a wrong room number written with the key cards. **Fail #9.**

CHAPTER 3: HAWAII

The next day, August 7th, our journey continued as we boarded the plane. We were in better spirits thanks to the absence of any issues. The aircraft soared through the skies with ease, carrying us closer to our destination. Upon arriving at Kona Airport in Hawaii, we disembarked swiftly, among the first passengers to step onto the island's soil.

As we made our way to the baggage pickup area, excitement mingled with anticipation. But my happiness quickly turned to worry when my checked luggage failed to materialize on the carousel. Keith was able to retrieve his luggage, but where was mine? Bewilderment was etched on our faces as we approached the Lost Baggage counter, seeking assistance. We provided the necessary details and discovered that my luggage had been mistakenly sent to Honolulu on a different flight! It was a disheartening realization, adding another disappointment to our growing list of mishaps. **Fail #10.**

Some may be wondering—if her luggage doesn't get returned to her, she wouldn't even have a wedding dress for the wedding! Well, good thing that I actually kept my wedding dress with me in my carry-on and my wedding shoes in Keith's. Whew. It's a major must-do for anyone who decides to have a destination wedding.

After settling the shipping arrangements for my luggage, Keith and I proceeded to board a shuttle bus which then took us to the car rental facility. The scorching sun beat down upon us, accentuating the challenges we've already faced on our journey at this point. A lengthy queue greeted us upon our arrival, prolonging our wait for the rental vehicle. We couldn't help but wonder what else could possibly go wrong.

Finally, after enduring a tedious two to three-hour wait, we were handed the keys to our rented car, a sleek black Jeep Wrangler. It was an unprecedented delay, possibly attributable to the lingering effects of the pandemic or a shortage of staff. Nevertheless, we were grateful to have a means of transportation for our island adventures.

Leaving the car rental place behind, we set off on our

drive to our eagerly awaited hotel, the Fairmont Orchid in Waimea, our home for the next seven days. The heat of the day was tempered by the stunning beauty of our surroundings, a dichotomy that mirrored our journey thus far. Despite the challenges, our spirits soared as we arrived at the hotel we had carefully chosen. Warm smiles greeted us at the reception, and we were treated to refreshing welcome drinks and live music. Gratitude filled us as we discovered that our wedding package had secured us an upgraded suite—a much-needed respite from our recent trials in the last twenty-four hours.

With plans to meet Keith's family for dinner that evening, we freshened up in our suite and prepared to head out. Keith had thoughtfully arranged for the valet to have our car ready when we returned to the hotel lobby. As we approached the lobby coming from our suite, the black Jeep Wrangler caught our attention right away, and we eagerly hopped in and set off toward the restaurant, a mere few minutes away.

Keith phoned his brother to inform him of our impending arrival, but as they spoke, another call interrupted him. It was the hotel valet, and confusion settled over us like a hazy fog. The realization struck that we had mistakenly taken someone else's car! "Well, that's why I thought the car seemed a little bit off," I said. With an embarrassed chuckle and a shake of our heads, we quickly turned around, driving back to the hotel. **Fail #11.**

Returning the incorrect vehicle, we encountered a family waiting in the lobby, their expressions a mix of frustration and impatience as they seemed in a rush to get to the airport with their luggage in tow. It became apparent that their own rental car had been usurped, causing an unforeseen delay in their travel plans. Our apologies were given, accompanied by the sincere apologies of the valet. The valet then guided them and us to our respective correct black Jeep Wranglers, grateful that the mix-up had been resolved amicably.

The day had been fraught with unexpected turns, yet we stayed resilient, ready to face whatever challenges lay ahead. Little did we know that our journey would continue to test our mettle, but we were determined to make the most of our Hawaiian adventure, embracing each twist and turn with unwavering spirit.

* * *

Waimea, Hawaii

After the preceding months of meticulous planning and jumping through the obstacles to get from Toronto to Hawaii, our dream of a beautiful, intimate wedding in Hawaii was finally becoming a reality on the lovely, sunny Tuesday of August 10, 2021.

The sun-kissed beaches and gentle ocean waves provided the perfect backdrop as we exchanged our vows in the presence of 16 of our closest family and friends (yes, far from the 60-80 we had originally planned), our minister Kahu Tom, plus many of our family and friends who joined us virtually over Zoom online. The air was filled with love and joy, our hearts overflowing with happiness as we embarked on this new chapter of our lives together.

Following the heartfelt celebration, Keith and I spent a few more days on the delightful Big Island of Hawaii. With its fascinating landscapes and laidback culture, the island beckoned us to explore its hidden treasures. From cascading waterfalls to wondrous volcanoes, we immersed ourselves in the awe-inspiring beauty that surrounded us.

Pololū Valley Beach

Days were filled with adventure and discovery as we drove through lush rainforests, hiked along the crystal-clear waters teeming with marine life, and witnessed the remnants of the fiery spectacle of molten lava flowing into the ocean, hiking past the driveable portion of the Chain of Craters Road in Hawaii Volcanoes National Park. Each experience deepened our connection not only with each other but also with the raw power and splendour of nature.

* * *

Sunset view from the top of Haleakala above the clouds

As our time on the Big Island drew to a close, Keith and I set our sights on the next leg of our journey on Saturday, August 14th—the breathtaking island of Maui. With its golden beaches and legendary sunsets, Maui held promises of enchantment and awe.

To our delight, our island-hopping escapade continued without any major hiccups. We enjoyed the exquisite beach just steps away from our hotel, The Westin Maui Resort & Spa. We found ourselves basking in the culinary delights of Mama's Fish House in Paia, indulging in delectable seafood dishes that danced upon our taste buds. The elegant ambiance of Lahaina Grill in Lahaina provided the perfect setting for a romantic evening, where we savoured exquisite meals and toasted to love and shared adventures.

And, of course, we couldn't resist the allure of the iconic Road to Hana (or Hana Highway), because what's a trip to Maui without navigating, at least once in your life, that incredible path that leads you through a haven of lush rainforests, countless waterfalls, and other hidden treasures? But that's not all—we didn't stop at the "end of the road." We pushed beyond the boundaries, venturing into the territory less travelled, where the path got narrower and the adrenaline surged higher. They say caution is advised, but our hearts yearned for adventure, and adventure we found, on those curvy, heart-thumping roads that held the secrets of the island's raw untamed beauty.

However, as the recurring theme of this journey thus far, another challenge did arise. One evening, as we made our way back to our hotel after exploring the far side of the island, we found ourselves caught in an unexpected traffic jam. The flow of cars came to a standstill, stretching out for miles ahead. An hour ticked by slowly, and our patience was tested as we waited for the traffic to ease.

It was then that we learned of a fire that had broken out, forcing a standstill at some point on the single highway through the island, and eventually allowing some traffic to crawl through. **Fail #12.**

Shave ice

Yet, even in the midst of the delay, Keith and I found solace in each other's company. We shared stories, laughed, and marvelled at the beauty of the island that surrounded us, understanding that sometimes, even the unexpected detours could lead to unexpected moments of connection and reflection. Seeing a small shave ice shop on the side of the road, we decided that we might as well stop by and enjoy the delicious frozen treat for the time being.

Finally, the traffic began to disperse, and we made our way back to our hotel. The experience served as a gentle reminder of the unpredictable nature of life's journey, where unforeseen circumstances could momentarily disrupt the smoothest of paths. But it also reinforced our resilience and ability to find joy even in the face of challenges.

As we settled into our room that night, a sense of gratitude washed over us. The memories we had created, the love we celebrate, and the adventures we had embarked upon were all part of a larger tapestry, woven with the threads of resilience, love, and the unwavering spirit of exploration.

And so, with hearts full of gratitude and anticipation, Keith and I drifted off to sleep, ready to embrace the next day of our remarkable journey.

CHAPTER 4: HAWAII TO LOS ANGELES TO TORONTO

The sun-kissed shores of Maui, Hawaii bid farewell to us as we embarked on our journey back to the North American mainland on Saturday, August 21, 2021. Our 1:00 p.m., Hawaii time flight from the island paradise to Los Angeles proved to be a smooth and uneventful affair, a brief respite from the trials and tribulations that had plagued our previous endeavours.

However, our relief was short-lived as we arrived at LAX at around 9:12 p.m., Pacific time (6:12 p.m., Hawaii time), only to be met with a dreaded announcement—our 11:35 a.m. Air Canada flight to Toronto the next day on August 22nd had been unceremoniously cancelled. **Fail #13.**

The realization sank in, and frustration tinged our weary souls. We were left stranded in a cloud of uncertainty, grappling with the consequences of yet another setback.

Adding to our mounting concerns, we soon discovered that our luggage was not set up to be automatically transferred by United Airlines onto the next flight leg. Weary with the news of yet another delay, we went on to retrieve our belongings. With hopeful hearts, we approached the airline staff, hoping for a glimmer of assistance to be rebooked onto the next flight home to Toronto.

To our dismay, the promise of immediate respite proved elusive. The staff explained that there were no other flights to Toronto on Sunday, August 22nd and that we'll have to spend an additional night in Los Angeles. What's more, a hotel voucher could not be provided right away, leaving us with no choice but to return the following morning to pick up the voucher for our accommodations.

With weariness etched on our faces, we contemplated another night of uncertainty and the toll it would take on us. Furthermore, we were supposed to get back to work at our day jobs on Monday, but now we would have to miss a day's work.

As if fate revelled in our plight, the compensation

offered by the airline added insult to injury. A mere $40 in food and beverage vouchers was presented to us—a paltry sum to sustain us in this hassled time. Our minds drifted to the contrast of the generosity exhibited by United Airlines just a couple of weeks ago, who had granted us $80 in similar circumstances. Slight resentment simmered beneath the surface as we grappled with this unfairness.

With luggage in tow, we hopped on a shuttle bus that would lead us to the Los Angeles Airport Marriott, our sanctuary for the night.

As we stepped into the lobby of the hotel, we felt a sense of relief wash over us. The comforting ambiance and warm welcome from the staff assured us that we were in for a well-deserved respite. The plush beds and luxurious amenities beckoned us, promising a night of blissful rest before we take on another day.

The following morning, Keith and I headed back to the airport eager to pick up the hotel voucher we were promised. With the voucher secured, we thought—why not make the most of our limited time here and explore this bustling city's charm? Carpe diem! Without hesitation, we hopped onto the shuttle bus that would lead us to the car rental facility, where freedom on wheels awaited.

Our first stop after getting our car rental was the

Sonesta Hotel, the airline's designated hotel for accommodations for our second night in the city. We dropped off our luggage and set off on our adventure for the day.

With our hearts and minds set on transforming our unforeseen extended stay into an adventure, we hit the road with a sense of determination coursing through our veins. Rodeo Drive in Beverly Hills beckoned, and we cruised along the glamorous street, soaking in the opulence that surrounded us. The allure of the high-end boutiques and designer shops lured us in, as we indulged in a bit of quick window shopping.

As the day turned into late afternoon, our appetites called for attention, and we treated ourselves to a sumptuous dinner that tantalized our taste buds. The flavours danced on our tongues, a celebration of the unexpected moments that had led us here.

Santa Monica Pier

With bellies satisfied, we headed out to our next destination, finding ourselves at the iconic Santa Monica Pier. The vibrant energy of the area enveloped us, the sights and sounds harmonizing in a symphony of excitement. We strolled along the pier, absorbing the carnival-like atmosphere, and took a moment to breathe in the salty ocean air that carried with it the promise of enchantment.

As the sun dipped below the horizon, painting the sky in hues of orange and pink, we witnessed an awe-inspiring sunset that mirrored the beauty of our impromptu escapade. The moment was magical, and we knew that these unexpected experiences were weaving their way into the tapestry of our journey.

We continued our coastal adventure, driving as close to the waterfront as we could toward Venice. The ocean's rhythm whispered tales of wanderers and dreamers, and we revelled in the spontaneity of the night.

As we returned to our hotel, exhaustion blended with contentment, a rewarding sensation that comes from seizing the day. Our unplanned extended stay had become an opportunity for discovery, for embracing the unknown and finding joy in the unexpected.

With grateful hearts, we settled in for the night taking our much-needed rest, knowing that our journey had taken a delightful turn. The beauty of life lies in its twists and turns, in the moments we never anticipated, and in the memories that linger long after the day is done.

The anticipated flight, scheduled for 11:35 a.m. the next day, Monday, August 23rd, carried the promise of progress. Yet, fate proved a fickle companion, as the departure time was delayed to 12:20 p.m. **Fail #14.**

With our patience strained, Keith and I clung to the belief that this setback would be the last.

In a brief moment of appeasement, Air Canada extended another $20 in food and beverage vouchers, a meager offering in the grand scheme of our tumultuous journey. Gratitude and frustration waged a battle within us as we accepted the meager concession, as we acknowledged that even the smallest gestures gave us some semblance of relief.

The hours dwindled as we languished in the airport's confines, each ticking minute a testament to our surprising perseverance. When we finally boarded our plane, we were filled with considerable calmness and comfort.

* * *

At last, the wheels of our aircraft kissed the ground at around 8:04 p.m., Eastern time at Toronto Pearson International Airport, our weary bodies longing for respite. Relief surged through our veins, a beacon amidst the chaos we had endured.

Our journey, however, was far from over. Customs became an arduous hurdle, stretching minutes into eternity as we awaited our turn. Finally, at 8:45 p.m., we emerged from the grasp of customs, weary but determined to reach the comforts of home.

I checked both the Uber and Lyft apps and decided to go with Lyft this time around since it was cheaper at this particular time. Summoning the last vestiges of energy, we got on our Lyft ride at 9:36 p.m., the final leg of our odyssey. Fatigue clung to our bones as we set off on the familiar route, the passing scenery a blur through bleary eyes. The hands of the clock ticked, seconds stretching into eternity, until, at 9:53 p.m., we arrived at the doorstep of our Humber Bay Shores condo.

Exhausted, we stepped into the embrace of home, grateful for the sanctuary it provided. This journey had tested our resilience, leaving us a little bit scarred yet renewed. We had traversed the treacherous seas of unexpected twists and turns, weathering the storm of cancellations, delays, and misplaced luggage. Each trial had tested our patience, strength, and resolve, but through it all, our bond had only grown stronger.

As we unpacked our bags, carefully placing each item back into its rightful place, a sense of closure washed over us. The physical remnants of our journey were safely returned, tangible reminders of the resilience we had throughout.

Reflecting on our arduous adventure, we found solace in the lessons learned along the way. We discovered the power of adaptability, embracing the unexpected with open arms and unwavering determination. We learned to find beauty in the midst of chaos, cherishing the fleeting moments of tranquility amidst the turbulence.

As we settled into the comfort of our own bed, our hearts filled with gratitude for the experiences we encountered, both triumphs and tribulations. Our journey had come to an end, but the memories forged during those tumultuous days would forever shape our perspectives. We tasted the bitter sting of disappointment, yet emerged stronger, armed with an unwavering belief in our ability to overcome.

With the dawn of a new day, we awoke to a world that held infinite possibilities. The echoes of our adventures lingered, reminding us that the path ahead was never certain, but with each step, we would continue to embrace the unknown.

As the pages turn, we eagerly await the unwritten chapters, ready to embark on new journeys, armed with the lessons learned, and fueled by the undying flame of wanderlust that burned within our souls. The world awaits, and we are ready to answer its call.

PART II

CHAPTER 5: PORTO TO LISBON

The trip to our destination wedding and back was not the first time Keith and I experienced some incredible travel misadventures.

Let's rewind a little bit back in time to Friday, September 28, 2018—a date that marked the beginning of an unforgettable European adventure. With eager hearts, wide smiles, and soaring spirits we bid farewell to Toronto at 9:15 p.m., our plane bound for the magnificent city of Rome, Italy. What an epic trip this is going to be!

Italy, the land of history, art, and delectable cuisine, welcomed us with open arms. From Rome to Florence and then Venice, we savoured every moment, basking in the rich tapestry of Italian culture that unfolded before us in the span of ten days. The ancient ruins whispered stories of bygone eras, while the Renaissance masterpieces painted a vivid picture of artistic brilliance. Each city offered its unique charm, leaving us in awe of Italy's grandeur.

The train was our mode of travel, whisking us from one Italian gem to another, weaving through picturesque landscapes, vineyards, and quaint villages. The rhythmic movement of the train wheels mirrored the excitement bubbling within us, as we eagerly anticipated the wonders that lay ahead.

But Italy was just the prologue of our odyssey. Soon, on Monday, October 8th, we boarded a plane and jetted off to the vibrant streets of Barcelona, Spain. The city's energy was infectious, and we immersed ourselves in its colourful culture. Strolling through Gaudi's architectural wonders, indulging in tapas and sweet treats, and enjoying the music wafting through the streets— Barcelona offered a sensory feast that left us intoxicated with life, even in just two short days.

City of Porto overlooking the Douro River

And then, the time came to make our way to Porto, Portugal on Wednesday, October 10th—the raison d'être for this whole trip, to witness the marriage and stand by my childhood best friend as her maid of honour within the next few days. As the plane descended upon Porto, our hearts swelled with joy and excitement. It would be five unforgettable days in Porto, a city that embraced us with open arms and unveiled its hidden treasures. The air was filled with the tantalizing aroma of local delicacies, tempting our taste buds at every turn. With hearts full of anticipation and joy, we revelled in the vibrant streets, relishing in the maze of alleyways that whispered tales of centuries gone by.

From the moment we arrived, Porto captivated us with its charm and unique character. Each day was a new adventure, a chance to uncover the city's secrets and enjoy its wines. As we meandered through the colourful neighbourhoods, we couldn't help but marvel at the stunning blend of old-world charm and modern innovation that defined this captivating city.

Porto's culinary delights were a feast for the senses. We savoured every morsel of the traditional Portuguese dishes, from the mouthwatering bacalhau to the heavenly pastel de nata. Each meal was a celebration of flavours, a delightful dance on our taste buds that left us craving for more.

As the days melted into one another, the excitement for the upcoming wedding of my dearest best friend of over two decades grew exponentially. We found ourselves eagerly counting down the hours, anxious to witness the union of two souls destined for each other.

Clérigos Church

The wedding day on Saturday, October 13th finally arrived, and Porto seemed to come alive with even more radiance. It was a tremendous honour to witness the celebration of love, friendship, and the beauty of life, surrounded by the picturesque beauty of Porto. As the vows were exchanged and tears of joy glistened in everyone's eyes, we were reminded of the precious bonds that withstand the test of time. It was nothing short of a fairy tale—a beautiful setting at the church and reception, love filling the air, and the echoes of laughter and music resonating among us.

The late-night festivities of the Portuguese wedding we attended meant we had only gotten a few hours of sleep that night, as the celebrations had continued throughout the night and into the early morning.

On Sunday, October 14th, the last day of our Europe trip, Keith and I set off on a thrilling adventure that began amidst a torrential downpour. We were running, desperately trying to catch the train as it barreled along the tracks, but it showed no signs of stopping as we had just missed it by more than 30 seconds. Keith jokingly urged me to signal the train to halt, which would be an obvious futile attempt as that doesn't really happen in real life… or does it? We found ourselves stranded, helplessly watching as the train disappeared into the distance, leaving us with no choice but to reschedule for the next one.

This unfortunate turn of events posed a challenge since even if we took the next train scheduled in two hours, and made it in time to board the plane, it jeopardized our ability to check in our luggage in time for our flight to Toronto from Lisbon, where our just-departed train was headed. Looking up the cost of separately sending our luggage through a luggage shipping service back to Toronto from Porto was exorbitant, in the thousands of dollars, which limited us from this option.

We contemplated taking our international flight the following day, but the airline's ticketing hours were inconveniently timed as by the time they opened, our flight would have already left. We also checked for the availability of local Porto to Lisbon flights that day, but unfortunately, there were none. Furthermore, we explored the option of renting a car one-way, which came with a price tag of 250 euros.

Trip details

UberX ride with Augusto

Oct 14 7:44AM

€241.88

🏷 Receipt

● Rua da Estação 2, 4300-273 Porto, Portugal   7:53AM

■ Aeroporto de Lisboa, Parque P1, 1700-111 Lisboa, Portugal   10:52AM

As we weighed our alternatives, we considered Uber as a potential solution. Initially, the Uber app quoted me around 340 euros, but after checking again 45 minutes later, I managed to find a more affordable option at 285 euros (the actual cost ended up being 241.88 euros), which was almost the same price as renting a car. Approaching the plan with a hint of skepticism, we quickly decided to book the ride, feeling a wave of relief when we found a willing driver who promptly arrived to pick us up.

With the initial mix-up of mistakenly entering "Camphana subway station" instead of "Camphana metro station" in the app, leading the driver to the wrong place to pick us up, our driver eventually found us, and we set off. The 300-kilometre journey from Porto to Lisbon was a silent one since our driver didn't speak English, and our attempts to communicate with the help of the Google Translate app were rather clumsy.

Who would have thought that we'd be taking an Uber for such a lengthy distance? Not us, that's for sure! But here we are on our most expensive Uber ride ever thus far.

On the road between the two cities, the landscape was marked by the aftermath of the recent hurricane Leslie that hit central Portugal. We observed numerous broken trees and damages, a testament to the storm's impact. I dozed off part of the way, but I'm glad that the ride was smooth otherwise.

Despite the challenges and hiccups, we felt grateful for the wonderful wedding experience and the opportunity to have explored several cities on this trip.

However, our misadventures weren't over yet. Rushing to the airport, we nearly missed the 12:50 p.m. flight, becoming some of the last passengers to board after it took us a while to get through security and customs. Fortunately, we made it, relieved to see that three other individuals were also boarding at that late hour. After the incredible day we had, we made it back to Toronto at 4:00 p.m., Eastern time (9:00 p.m., Western European time), both in one piece.

Looking back on our 17-day vacation, it was truly an incredible experience filled with unforgettable moments. The wedding and the journey itself had their fair share of surprises and obstacles, but they added to the overall excitement of the trip. Now, we eagerly await our next adventure, which we hope will be just as remarkable.

CHAPTER 6: REVELSTOKE TO BANFF

On Sunday, March 17, 2019, Keith and I found our adventurous selves on an exciting drive from Revelstoke, British Columbia back to Banff, Alberta.

Canadian Rockies (Rocky Mountains)

But first, let me take you back to a few hours earlier. Before the sun began its ascent over the majestic peaks of Banff, we eagerly set out on yet another thrilling escapade, leaving the Delta Banff hotel, our abode for the last few days. Our destination? Revelstoke Mountain Resort, a legendary haven for ski enthusiasts, beckoning us with the promise of unforgettable adventures.

Having already relished the slopes of Lake Louise Ski Resort in the preceding days, we yearned for new horizons to conquer. Revelstoke stood tall, challenging us with its awe-inspiring reputation—boasting the longest vertical descent of any ski resort in North America, an adrenaline-pumping 1,710-metre plunge into exhilaration.

The anticipation swirled within us as we set off on the journey, the crisp mountain air invigorating our spirits and fueling our excitement. The road ahead unfurled like a ribbon of adventure, winding through breathtaking landscapes that seemed to come straight out of a winter fairy tale.

As we neared our destination, Revelstoke emerged before us like a beacon of winter wonder. Its snow-covered peaks reached for the skies, promising an unparalleled skiing experience that would etch itself into our memories forever.

Gearing up with our skis, we stood at the base of the

mountain, gazing upwards in awe. The snow-laden trails beckoned us, inviting us to ascend and embrace the challenge of conquering Revelstoke's awe-inspiring vertical drop.

With each ascent on the chairlift, our excitement grew, mingled with a touch of exhilarating nervousness. The anticipation was palpable as we ascended higher and higher, feeling a surge of adrenaline coursing through our veins.

And then, at the summit, we stood in awe of the breathtaking panorama that stretched before us. It was as if we had reached the pinnacle of the world, with snowcapped mountains and untamed wilderness stretching as far as the eye could see.

The moment we had been waiting for had arrived. We took a deep breath, absorbing the breathtaking view, before we plunged into the vast expanse of snow beneath us. The descent was an exhilarating dance of pure joy (and tears for me) skiing down the longest vertical drop in North America, especially as I unintentionally led us down a black diamond trail. For the uninitiated, a black diamond ski run is one of the more difficult slopes relative to the other runs around it made for advanced skiers, with a gradient of 40% or higher. With every glide, adrenaline surged through our veins as we weaved through the powdery paradise.

After an amazing day of skiing, the clock struck 3:30 p.m., Pacific time (4:30 p.m., Mountain time) as we set off, our car rental joining the flow of traffic moving steadily along the winding roads in the Pacific time zone. The anticipation of the journey ahead filled the air with excitement as we would be seeing the breathtaking snowcapped mountain scenery between B.C. and Alberta on the drive back.

As we continued down the road, we noticed something intriguing—a small avalanche in the area. It piqued our curiosity, and we couldn't wait to capture it on video later. But beneath our excitement, a nagging concern lingered—the snowy conditions that lay ahead. We hoped that the road wouldn't be obstructed, causing us delays or closures.

The Google Maps app estimated that we'd reach our hotel by 7:35 p.m., Mountain time, assuming there were no unforeseen road closures due to avalanches. It meant we had approximately three more hours of driving ahead, but the unpredictability of the weather had us on edge. Would there be unexpected stops on our path? Only time would tell.

Remnants of an avalanche on the road side

After a while, we witnessed an avalanche coming down just halfway across the road, but thankfully we managed to pass through shortly after it happened.

It was quite a scene on the road. People were swerving in front of us to avoid the aftermath of the avalanche. There were also some smaller avalanches with lighter snow, in big chunks coming down towards the ground.

Although we didn't witness any major avalanches firsthand, we did see the remnants of one that had affected one car.

Suddenly, at 6:22 p.m., Mountain time (5:22 p.m., Pacific time), our plans hit a snag. Avalanche control was underway, and the roads wouldn't reopen until 8:00 p.m., Mountain time. Keith tells me that avalanche control is a blasting done to trigger avalanches. The Army is involved, and they shoot artillery pieces at the avalanche-prone areas to proactively trigger controlled avalanches. These controlled avalanches are meant to keep us safe on the road.

Rather than waste time sitting idle in our cars, we decided to make the most of the situation. We exited at the small town of Golden and found refuge at a Husky restaurant, enjoying a leisurely dinner while we waited for the all-clear signal.

The journey had its challenges, yet it was also filled with wonder and fascination. Conversations with the restaurant staff revealed tales of past incidents, including being snowed in for days. Despite the obstacles, the idea of exploring the area further intrigued us, especially with the tempting allure of a nearby ski hill.

By 8:14 p.m., we were back on the road after overcoming the road closure and dealing with some car troubles. Our vehicle had overheated earlier, but luckily, it was running smoothly now. The night had been a rollercoaster of experiences, but we soldiered on, eagerly anticipating our arrival at the hotel, which was now expected around 9:15 p.m., Mountain time.

The traffic was moving at a snail's pace, about 10 kilometres per hour. It was a bit backed up, but hopefully, we would reach our hotel before 10:00 p.m. We still had about 140 kilometres to go on this slow drive on the Trans-Canada Highway.

In the middle of our adventurous road trip, just when we thought we had overcome all the hurdles for the day, fate had another surprise in store for us. As we approached a curve on the road, about 20 minutes past Golden, our car's engine suddenly started overheating. We pulled over, feeling a mix of frustration and concern, and popped the hood to assess the damage. After letting it cool down, we tried restarting the engine, but it stubbornly refused to cooperate.

Feeling defeated, I called CAA reaching out for help, explaining our stranded situation. After what felt like an eternity, a CAA tow truck finally arrived, providing a glimmer of hope. However, the reality sank in that towing us all the way to Banff that night was impossible, given the temporary road closures due to avalanche control.

Instead, the driver offered us a ride back to the town of Golden, towing our vehicle with us. There seemed to be little he could do to get our car fixed immediately, so the plan was to take us back to Banff across the province border in the morning.

Exhausted from the rollercoaster of events, we checked into a simple yet comfortable motel in Golden for the night. Grateful that we were at least safe with a place to rest, we let the weight of the day's trials slip away as we drifted off to sleep.

The following day brought a glimmer of hope—thankfully, with my CAA Plus membership (which I highly recommend), the 140-kilometre tow cost from Golden to Banff was covered for free, with the exception of a minimal inter-province transport fee. With renewed optimism, the CAA driver promptly drove us and our car back to Banff as promised, as if determined to make amends for the challenges we had faced the day before.

In the afternoon of Monday, March 18th, we continued our drive from Banff to Calgary. The previous night's escapade seemed like a distant memory as we glided along the highway. Our car rental, a 2019 Nissan Murano with only 600 kilometres on it, had encountered some mysterious issues, but for now, it was performing well.

With a few hours before our flight back to Toronto, scheduled for 8:10 p.m., we decided to seize the opportunity and explore Calgary. It was the perfect way to round off our trip—a blend of adventure, trials, and delightful discoveries.

In the end, this trip taught us that the true essence of the journey lay in embracing the unpredictability of the road, appreciating the beauty of nature, and cherishing the camaraderie forged along the way. Each twist and turn brought new stories and memories, creating a tale of an unforgettable adventure that we would carry with us for a lifetime.

SPREADING LOVE AND HOPE

Love triumphs over adversity. The essence of true love lies not in a flawless journey, but in the way two hearts face challenges hand in hand. With every delay and detour, especially if you can find humour in whatever life throws at you, your commitment to your significant other is made stronger.

I hope this memoir has given you a renewed sense of hope and belief in the resilience of love and the power of never giving up on challenges that come your way. By letting other readers know how this extraordinary journey touched your heart, you are helping me spread joy, laughter, and hope with them.

When you leave your honest thoughts about this book on Amazon and/or Goodreads—even with just a couple of lines, not only are you supporting me and my written work, but you also become a part of the shared journey of love and hope—thank you for your support!

SCAN THE QR CODE TO LEAVE A REVIEW

DELAYS, DETOURS, AND I DO

ABOUT THE AUTHOR

Anna Saldivar Turpin is a Filipino-Canadian currently living in Montreal, Quebec after having Toronto, Ontario as her home for 15 years and Bacolod, Philippines in her younger years. She is a passionate joiner of many things and an avid adventurer, with an insatiable wanderlust that has taken her to breathtaking destinations across the world. She weaves her real-life experiences and heartfelt emotions into captivating narratives that resonate with readers. When she's not writing or working her day job, you can find her exploring new places, going on adventures locally or otherwise, savouring local cuisines, and cherishing moments with her husband, Keith.

If you want to get in touch, you can reach out to her through the following social media channels:

𝕏 x.com/annasaldivar
instagram.com/annasaldivar
linkedin.com/in/annasaldivar
youtube.com/annaisabelsaldivar

www.ingramcontent.com/pod-product-compliance
Lightning Source LLC
Chambersburg PA
CBHW070931120626
46546CB00004B/1387

* 9 7 8 1 9 9 8 0 9 9 0 6 1 *